Christmas Carols
For Trumpet With
Piano Accompaniment
Sheet Music
Book 1

Michael Shaw

Music Arrangements. All Christmas Carol arrangements in this book by **Michael Shaw Copyright © 2015**

ISBN: 1515398277
ISBN-13: 978-1515398271

www.mikesmusicroom.co.uk

Contents

Introduction

Away In A Manger: Trumpet   1

Away In A Manger: Trumpet & Piano   2

While Shepherds Watched: Trumpet   4

While Shepherds Watched: Trumpet & Piano   5

The First Noel: Trumpet   7

The First Noel: Trumpet & Piano   8

Good King Wenceslas: Trumpet   10

Good King Wenceslas: Trumpet & Piano   11

The Holly And The Ivy: Trumpet   13

The Holly And The Ivy: Trumpet & Piano   14

Hark The Herald Angels Sing: Trumpet   16

Hark The Herald Angels Sing: Trumpet & Piano   17

O Come All Ye Faithful: Trumpet   19

O Come All Ye Faithful: Trumpet & Piano   20

We Wish You A Merry Christmas: Trumpet   22

We Wish You A Merry Christmas: Trumpet & Piano   23

Silent Night: Trumpet   25

Silent Night: Trumpet & Piano   26

Deck The Halls: Trumpet   28

Deck The Halls: Trumpet & Piano   29

About The Author   32

Introduction

The sheet music in this book has been arranged for Trumpet. There are two versions of every piece in this book. The first version is a Trumpet only arrangement, the second version is a Trumpet and piano accompaniment arrangement. Both versions are for beginners and easy to play. The piano parts in this book can be played on a piano, keyboard or organ.

Versions Of This Book For Other Instruments

As well as playing duets with piano in this book you can also play together in a duet or ensemble with other instruments with a sheet music book for that instrument.

To get a book for your instrument choose from the Christmas Carols With Piano Accompaniment Book 1 series. Instruments in this series include, Clarinet, Flute, Trombone, Alto Saxophone, Tenor Saxophone, French Horn and Trumpet. Please check out my author page on Amazon to view these books.

Author Page US
amazon.com/Michael-Shaw/e/B00FNVFJGQ/

Author Page UK
amazon.co.uk/Michael-Shaw/e/B00FNVFJGQ/

Away In A Manger

Trumpet

Traditional

Trumpet in B♭

Away In A Manger

Trumpet & Piano

Traditional

While Shepherds Watched Their Flocks

Trumpet

Traditional

Trumpet in B♭

Tpt.

Tpt.

Tpt.

Tpt.

While Shepherds Watched Their Flocks

Trumpet & Piano

Traditional

The First Noel

Trumpet

Traditional

The First Noel
Trumpet & Piano

Traditional

Good King Wenceslas

Traditional

Trumpet

Trumpet in B♭

Tpt.

Tpt.

Tpt.

Tpt.

Tpt.

Good King Wenceslas

Traditional

Trumpet & Piano

The Holly And The Ivy

Trumpet

Traditional

The Holly And The Ivy

Trumpet & Piano

Traditional

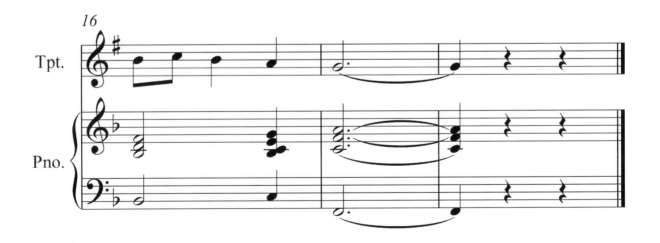

Hark The Herald Angels Sing

Trumpet

Mendelssohn

Trumpet in B♭

Tpt.

Tpt.

Tpt.

Tpt.

Tpt.

Hark The Herald Angels Sing

Trumpet & Piano

Mendelssohn

O Come All Ye Faithful

Trumpet

John Francis Wade

Trumpet in B♭

Tpt.

Tpt.

Tpt.

Tpt.

Tpt.

O Come All Ye Faithful

Trumpet & Piano

John Francis Wade

We Wish You A Merry Christmas

Trumpet

Traditional

We Wish You a Merry Christmas

Trumpet & Piano

Traditional

Silent Night
Trumpet

Traditional

Trumpet in B♭

5

Tpt.

10

Tpt.

15

Tpt.

20

Tpt.

Silent Night
Trumpet & Piano

Traditional

Deck The Halls

Trumpet

Traditional

Trumpet in B♭

Tpt.

Tpt.

Tpt.

Tpt.

Tpt.

Deck The Halls

Trumpet & Piano

Traditional

About the Author

Mike works as a professional musician and keyboard music teacher. Mike has been teaching piano, electronic keyboard and electric organ for over thirty years and as a keyboard player worked in many night clubs and entertainment venues.

Mike has also branched out in to composing music and has written and recorded many new royalty free tracks which are used worldwide in TV, film and internet media applications. Mike is also proud of the fact that many of his students have gone on to be musicians, composers and teachers in their own right.

You can connect with Mike at:

Facebook
facebook.com/keyboardsheetmusic

Soundcloud
soundcloud.com/audiomichaeld

YouTube
youtube.com/user/pianolessonsguru

I hope this book has helped you with your music, if you have received value from it in any way, then I'd like to ask you for a favour: would you be kind enough to leave a review for this book on Amazon? It'd be greatly appreciated!

Thank You
Michael Shaw

Made in the USA
San Bernardino, CA
20 October 2015